A First Look at Art

Families

Ruth Thomson

CHELSEA CLUBHOUSE
An Imprint of Chelsea House Publishers
A Haights Cross Communications Company
Philadelphia

This edition first published in 2004 in the United States of America by Chelsea Clubhouse, a division of Chelsea House Publishers and a subsidiary of Haights Cross Communications.

A Haights Cross Communications Company

Chelsea Clubhouse
1974 Sproul Road, Suite 400
Broomall, PA 19008-0914
www.chelseahouse.com

Library of Congress Cataloging-in-Publication Data applied for. ISBN 0-7910-7946-5

First published in the UK in 2003 by
Ⓒ Chrysalis Children's Books
The Chrysalis Building, Bramley Road,
London W10 6SP

Copyright © Chrysalis Children's Books, an imprint of Chrysalis Books Group, plc 2003
Text Copyright © Ruth Thomson 2003
Illustrator: Linda Francis
Photographer: Steve Shott
Consultant: Erika Langmuir, formerly head of education at the National Gallery, London

The author and publishers would like to thank the following people for their contributions to this book: Hazel Mills and pupils at Lady Bay Primary School and Elizabeth Emerson.

Printed in China

Picture acknowledgements

Front Cover: Scala, Florence, The Art Institute of Chicago 1990; 4: National Gallery, London; 5: Collection of Mississippi Museum of Art; 6/7: Courtesy of the Woolgar Family, Firle Place, Sussex; 10/11: Scala, London/MOMA/© Kahlo Estate; 11: © Kahlo Estate; 14: Courtesy of the Robert. B. Mayer Family Collection/ ©Escobar Marisol/VAGA, New York/DACS, London 2003; 15: Reproduced by permission of the Henry Moore Foundation; 18/19: ©Photo RMN/Gérard Blot; 22: Scala, Florence, The Art Institute of Chicago 1990; 23: National Portrait Gallery, London; 27: Bridgeman Art Library/ ©DVID Hockney.

Contents

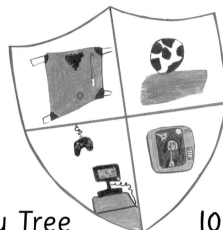

FAMILIES FOREVER

Throughout history, artists have portrayed all kinds of families – large and small, rich and poor, happy and sad, old and young. In this book you'll see a selection of family pictures. You will find out what inspired the artists and learn about their techniques. There are also questions to help you look at the works in detail and ideas for creating your own family **portraits** and sculptures.

◉ You'll find answers to the questions and information about the artists on pages 30-31.

Arty Tips

✬ Look for Arty Tips boxes that suggest handy techniques and materials to use in your own work.

Picture Hunt

✬ Picture Hunt boxes suggest other artists and artworks that you might like to find.

The Graham Children
William Hogarth
1742
(63.2 x 71.3 inches)

Family meanings

Artists portray families for different reasons. Hogarth painted the children on the left for their rich parents. The baby died while the picture was being made, so Hogarth included symbols, such as flowers and fruit, as reminders of the shortness of life.

Lawrence's painting, on the right, is not a portrait of one particular family. It represents the artist's belief that all people should live in harmony. Lawrence shows people of different races working together. The happy family links hands and all walk with the same foot forward.

Spotting clues

When you look at family portraits, think about what they mean. Study the **pose** of each figure. Does one person stand out more than the rest? If so, why? What does the setting say about the family's lifestyle?

The Builders
Jacob Lawrence
1974
(30 x 22.1 inches)

Reading relationships

See what you can tell about the family relationships. Do people touch one another? Do they turn their heads toward or away from one another? Do the shapes and colors of their clothes match or contrast?

John, Count of Nassau-Siegen, and His Family

Anthony Van Dyck

1634 (9.6 x 8.7 feet)

Before photography was invented, rich people asked well-known artists to paint their family portraits. These hung on display in their grand houses. Artists made sure they presented the family as impressively as possible, showing off their great wealth and status.

● Search for some clues that show this family's importance:

● their **coat of arms**

● the carved names of each person

● expensive clothes made of silk, satin, lace, and velvet

● rich textiles – tapestries, curtains, and rugs

● fine jewelry

Family relationships

Family portraits often looked to the future. They emphasized the importance of the first-born son, who would take on the family name and property. Notice how the pose and placing of these parents and children give clues about their relationships. The important-looking man and his wife are joined on a raised platform by their son and **heir.**

● How does the father indicate that the son is his heir?

● What can you guess about the boy's character from the way he is standing?

● Which is the oldest daughter? What clues tell you this?

FAMILY MATTERS

Our place

What is the place like where you and your family belong? How would you show it in a picture?

◉ Draw portraits of people in your family. Glue them down the side of a large sheet of colored, stiff paper.

Cassie, age 8

Maisie, age 8

Adam, age 9

◉ On another piece of paper, draw several images that represent your particular place. Choose things that are important to you.

◉ Glue this picture next to your family portraits.

Arty Tip

✤ Why not repeat your favorite images to form a pattern? Trace your drawing, or cut a simple shape into a potato, dip it in paint, and use it to print.

Surprising photos

Take some photographs of your family around your home or out and about. When you look at them, you may be surprised to see what they show about relationships in your family.

Joanna, age 8

Daisy, age 13

Family coat of arms

Make a family coat of arms, with clues about the activities and hobbies of people in your family.

◉ On stiff paper, draw a crest shape (see examples below). Cut it out.

◉ Divide the crest into four panels by drawing colored lines.

◉ Think of a picture clue for each person and draw it in one of the panels. If there are more than four people in your family, put more than one clue in each panel. If there are fewer, you could include pets, cousins, or even friends.

Examples of picture clues might be:

dog or cat........ paw print or bowl
travel.............. car, train, or airplane
gardening........ flower or watering can
cooking............. pan or spoon
baby................ bottle, rattle, or teddy

What others can you think of?

Becky, age 7

Ayaz, age 7, and Duncan, age 9

Mollie, age 8

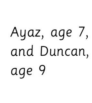

Picture Hunt

✫ Look for crests in pictures of grand and royal families. The colors and symbols each have a meaning – a bear symbolizes strength, a lion is a sign of bravery, and fur is a mark of dignity. Red is the color of a warrior, purple is royal, and blue symbolizes loyalty.

A FAMILY TREE

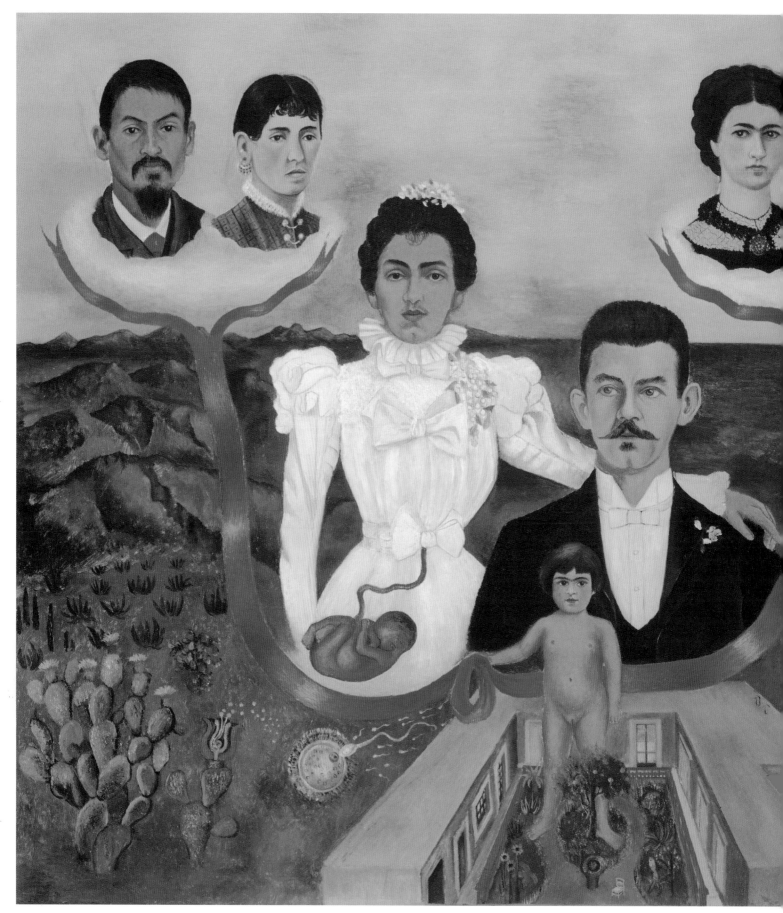

My Grandparents, My Parents, and I (Family Tree)
Frida Kahlo
1936 (12.1 x 13.7 inches)

A **family tree** is a way to show how family members of different **generations** are linked. Here, Frida Kahlo shows us how she is related to her parents and her two sets of grandparents.

◉ What has Frida used to link the people in her family tree? Why do you think it is red?

Frida and her home

Frida has painted herself as a two-year old, standing in the patio of the house where she was born. It was built by her father in the suburbs of Mexico City.

Frida's parents

The portraits of Frida's parents are based on their wedding photograph (*right*). The fuzzy cloud effect in the two floating portraits of her grandparents was inspired by this photo, too.

◉ What differences can you see between the photograph of Frida's parents and their painted portraits?

Frida's grandparents

Frida's mother had Mexican parents, but her father's family came from Germany. Notice how Frida suggests where her grandparents came from. Her Mexican grandparents hover over the rugged, dry land of Mexico, and her German relatives float above the ocean.

◉ Who is the strongest character in the painting? How do you think Frida felt about this person?

Wedding Photograph of Frida Kahlo's Parents 1898

FAMILY TIES

Draw your own family tree

Draw a family tree that shows the links between you and several generations of your family.

your mother or stepmother's parents

your father or stepfather's parents

your mother and father or stepmother or stepfather

you and your sister(s) or brother(s)

Becky, age 7

◉ Starting with yourself, draw pictures of your family, with people of each generation one above the other.

◉ Link the people together with lines to show how they are are connected.

A photographic family tree

If you have old photographs of your relatives, use them to make a family tree.

◉ Ask someone to take pictures of you, matching the poses of the old photos.

◉ Scan or make photocopies of the old photos. Use them side by side with your photos to make a decorated family tree.

Picture Hunt

✫ Look at pictures that show other ways of representing several generations, such as **She Ain't Holding Them Up: She's Holding On: Some English Rose!** by Sonia Boyce and **Many Happy Returns of the Day** by William Powell Frith.

Indi, age 11

A family tree collage

Make a **collage** tree decorated with pictures of your family.

◉ Paint or stick separate portraits of people in your family on plain fabric.

◉ Glue ribbon or lace around each picture to make a fancy frame.

Sadie, age 10

Jiang Jiang, age 10

Jessica, age 10

Eden, age 11

Sadie, Jiang Jiang, Holly, Naomi, and Jessica, age 10, and Frances and Eden, age 11

Frances, age 11

◉ Cut out a tree trunk from brown fabric.

◉ Stick on fabric branches and leaves.

◉ Glue your pictures onto the tree, with you at the bottom, your parents above, your grandparents above them, and so on.

◉ Link the generations with colored cord or string, rick-rack, wool, or ribbon.

Arty Tips

✩ You could glue on embroidery thread, wool, or cotton wool for hair and beards.

✩ Decorate the frames with sequins and cut-out flowers. Try to create an old-fashioned look for the older generations.

MODEL FAMILIES

These two sculptures of families are larger than life. Neither portrays a particular family. Instead, both express an *idea* about families.

◉ What immediate differences can you *see* between these two families? Compare the poses and the arrangements of the figures. Compare the different materials.

The Family
Marisol
1963
(6.6 feet high)

All dressed up

Marisol's sculpture (*left*) pokes fun at a family that has dressed up to go for a stroll. Perhaps they mean to be serious, but Marisol makes this a joke.

◉ How does Marisol show the serious nature of the family?

◉ What differences are there in the way Marisol's mother and father are sculpted?

◉ What's odd about the girl with the doll and the feet in the buggy?

Mixed media

Marisol mixed ready-made objects with painted blocks of wood and wood carving.

◉ Which are ready-made objects? What has been carved or painted on wood?

Family togetherness

Henry Moore sculpted this family group soon after he became a father himself. It reflects his own idea of being part of a family.

Moore first made a small model of the sculpture out of plaster. Then he had it enlarged in bronze.

◉ How do you think Moore felt about being a father?

◉ How has Moore shown the closeness between the two parents?

◉ Which parts of the parents has Moore simplified or exaggerated? What effect does this create?

Family Group
Henry Moore
1948-9 (5 feet high)

SCULPTING THE FAMILY

A clay family

Sculpt your own idea of what a family is.
⊙ Shape each person from modeling clay.
⊙ Decide how the people feel about one another and show these feelings in their poses. They might hug one another or stand apart. They might lean toward or away from one another.

Arty Tips

✧ Keep hands and faces simple. Tilt, twist, or bend parts of the figures to suggest movement and expression.

✧ Exaggerate the size of the feet of standing people so they stay upright.

Ayesha, age 7

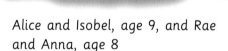

Alice and Isobel, age 9, and Rae and Anna, age 8

Louis, Christopher, and Alex, age 9, and Charlie and Farhan, age 8

Picture Hunt

✧ Compare other family sculptures, such as **The Man-Child** by Frank Dobson, **Mother and Child** by Barbara Hepworth, and **Woman with Baby Carriage** by Pablo Picasso.

✧ Look at sculpted figures by Julio Gonzáles, Joan Miró, and Alberto Giacometti to discover some other sculptural techniques.

A wire family

Use thin aluminum wire or plastic-coated garden wire to make a dancing family sculpture.

◉ Bend and twist long pieces of wire to shape the figures' heads and bodies.

◉ Wrap around more wire for the arms, legs, and hair.

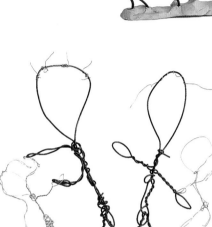

Jazmin and Tessa, age 8

◉ Join some of the people together by the hands.

◉ Stand your sculptures up on a base of modeling clay.

◉ Adjust their poses to create a feeling of action and liveliness.

Alex, age 9

Alice, age 9

Funny families

Create a funny family using clean, empty plastic bowls and lids, cardboard tubes and boxes, egg cartons, buttons, and other junk.

◉ Use colored pipe cleaners for hair, arms, and legs. Add peel-off stickers for some of the features, as well as for decoration.

Rubia, Isobel, and Sophie, age 9, and Hannah, age 8

Christopher and Louis, age 9, and Declan, Adrian, and Charlie, age 8

The Bellelli Family Edgar Degas
1858-67 (6.6 x 8.2 feet)

The arrangement of the figures in family portraits can say a lot about their feelings. Here, Degas shows the misery in the family of his aunt, Laure Bellelli. Laure's father, whose portrait hangs on the wall by her head, had recently died. Laure and her two daughters, Giovanna and Giulia, are dressed in black clothes for mourning.

◉ What clues in the room suggest that the family is quite well off?

A family split

Laure and her husband, Gennaro, were not happy together. Degas used lines and shapes to emphasize the split in the family.

Notice how the sides of the mirror and fireplace and the table leg create a dividing line between Gennaro and his family. The armchair also encloses Gennaro, cutting him off from the rest of the room.

Poses and glances

Degas gives more clues about relationships in the family through everyone's posture and expression. He varies the angle of each person's face and eyes to help get the message across.

◉ How would you describe Laure's pose and expression?

◉ Where is each person looking? What effect do their gazes have on the image of the family as a whole?

◉ How does Degas suggest that Giulia (sitting on the chair) might be torn between her two parents?

Cool colors

Artists can use color to suggest moods. Here, Degas has used a variety of cold blues and grays to suggest gloom and sadness.

The fire and the candle are not lit, so there is no warmth in the room. Even the light from the window, reflected in the mirror, feels chilly.

IN THE MOOD

Expressions

Practice drawing faces with all sorts of expressions. Use these examples to help you. Notice how the shape and position of the eyes, nose, and mouth change. The closeness or space between the features also helps to create some very different expressions.

happy	sad	angry	frightened	thoughtful

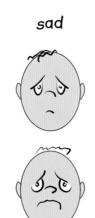

What a feeling!

Draw a family portrait, giving each person an expression and pose that suits his or her personality and feelings.

Jamie, age 8

Arron, age 8

Arty Tip

✫ Before you draw, think about how you feel when you are sad, angry, or frightened and make a face in the mirror. Remember your face and your feelings when you start drawing.

Family life

Draw or paint a picture of a family spending time together. You might choose an everyday scene. Or you could show the family dressed up for a celebration, going to the movies, or playing in a park.

◉ Add extra details, such as your pets or favorite things that you own, do, or wear.

Evie, age 6

Mary Beth, age 8

Flora, age 8

Duncan, age 9

◉ Try to use colors that express the mood of the occasion — bright colors tend to look happy and lively, while dull colors feel serious or sad.

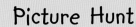

Picture Hunt

✭ Look at pictures that show family life, such as **Pianist and Checkers Players** by Henri Matisse, **Hide and Seek** by James-Jacques-Joseph Tissot, **Portrait of a Family Making Music** by Peter de Hooch, and **Sunday Afternoon** by Fernando Botero.

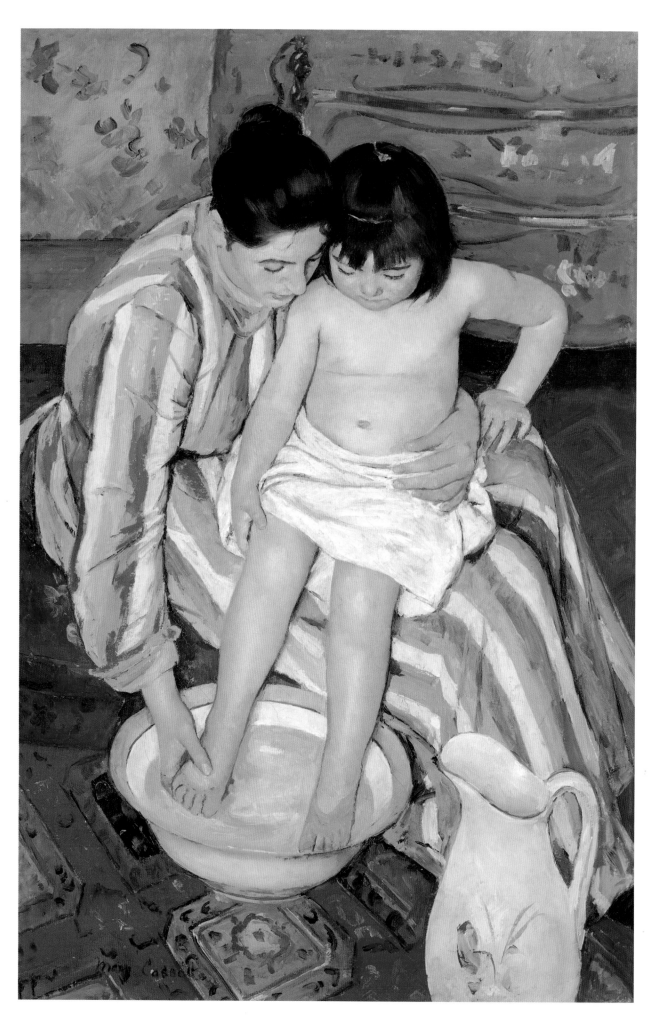

Sometimes, as in these two paintings, artists concentrate on the relationship between just one parent and child.

◉ What are the first differences you notice between the two parent-child relationships pictured here?

Mother and daughter

Cassatt often painted tender, everyday scenes of mothers and children. Her picture on the left was painted at a time when few homes had running water. To make the scene look unposed, Cassatt painted it as if watching from above. Neither figure appears to have noticed the painter, as they both look down at the child's foot in the basin.

◉ How does Cassatt show affection between the mother and child?

Father and son

By contrast, Sir Walter Raleigh and his son (*right*) stare boldly out at us. This full-length portrait is a public display of power and ambition. Raleigh was a famous English soldier, explorer, and poet, who lived at the time of Queen Elizabeth I. He is said to have introduced tobacco and potatoes to Britain.

Raleigh's stiff pose, with hand on hip, was used by Elizabethan artists to suggest a tough, confident man of action.

◉ What clue shows Raleigh was a soldier?
◉ How would you describe Raleigh's looks and character?
◉ Why do you think Raleigh's son copies his father's pose?

The Bath
Mary Cassatt
1891-92 (39.5 x 26 inches)

Sir Walter Raleigh
unknown
1602 (78.5 x 50.1 inches)

ME AND YOU

Make the connection

Think how you might show a connection between a parent and child in a picture. It could be a warm hug, a game of football, a shopping trip, or even an argument.

◉ Make pencil sketches of your ideas. Think about how near or far apart you will place the two people and whether or not they will be looking at each other.

◉ Paint a picture of one of your ideas.

Holly, age 10

Flora, age 8

Tallissa, age 9

Jodi, age 5

Elly, age 8

Picture Hunt

✧ Compare other parent and child paintings, such as **The Cradle** by Berthe Morisot, **The Sick Child** by Edvard Munch, **Augustine Roulin with Marcelle** by Vincent Van Gogh, **Portrait of Alexander J. Cassatt and His Son, Robert Kelso Cassatt** by Mary Cassatt, **Vicomtesse Vilain XIII and Her Daughter** by Jacques-Louis David, and any pictures of the Madonna and Child.

Dress to impress

Sir Walter Raleigh and his son dressed in their best outfits for their portraits.

◉ Imagine an artist is going to paint a portrait of you with one of your parents. Design outfits for both of you to wear. They can be as wacky as you like!

Kate, age 9

William, age 10

Beth, age 7

Remi, age 10

Ewen, age 10

Catherine, age 5

Sam, age 11

Alex, age 7

Arty Tips

✫ Use repeating colors for both people if you want to emphasize the links between them. Use contrasting colors and shapes to stress differences.

✫ You could create a collage by adding decoration such as fabric, ribbon, buttons, glitter, or beads.

THE FAMILY ALBUM

A century ago, few people owned cameras. Having a family photo taken was a big event. People dressed in their best clothes and went to a photographer's **studio**.

Family in focus

Family photos were carefully composed to make everyone look their best. They often included props, such as painted backdrops, velvet drapes, and fancy chairs.

◉ Compare these two family photographs:
• How did the photographers make sure that everyone in the family could be seen clearly?
• Who is the focus of each photo? How can you tell?
• How did the photographers link the family members?

Painterly poses

Many photographs were inspired by painted portraits.
◉ What similarities are there between the photograph on the right and the family portrait shown on page 4?

Family photographs taken at portrait photographers' studios

**George, Blanche,
Celia, Albert,
and Percy**
David Hockney
1983
(43.7 x 46.5 inches)

A photomontage

This picture is made from lots of color photographs. Hockney took a variety of close-up shots of this family in their sitting room with their cats. He overlapped the photos and stuck them together to make a collage, called a **photomontage**.

From start to finish

Hockney's arrangement of the photos shows the family members at several different moments in time. Notice how their heads, bodies, and hands shift and their expressions change from one photo to the next. Look at the cats as well.

◉ How many photographs are there of each person's head?

◉ How has Hockney included himself and the rest of the room in the picture?

◉ What differences are there between this family picture and the old ones taken in photographic studios?

FAMILY SNAPSHOTS

Strike a pose!

Take your own specially posed family photographs. Think about these things before you start:

◉ Will you take the photos inside or outside your house or elsewhere?

◉ How will people pose?

◉ Will you take photos close up (just faces) or from farther away?

◉ Will people dress up nicely?

◉ Will you ask people to look at the camera or at one another?

◉ Will they be smiling or serious?

◉ Will you include cousins, uncles, aunts, grandparents, or any pets?

Andrew, age 5

Christopher, age 9

Rachel, age 9

Jamie, age 8

Frances, age 11

Emile, age 5

Arty Tips

✧ If you want to capture people's characters in the photo, tell them to act naturally and don't warn them when you're about to take the picture. Take several "surprise" shots.

✧ If you want to be in the photos, ask a friend to take the shot once you've fixed the pose. Or use a camera with a self-timer.

People puzzle

Make a photomontage.

◉ Use a copier to enlarge a photo to fill the full page.

◉ Make several copies of it.

◉ Cut each copy into 2-inch (4-centimeter) squares.

◉ Arrange the squares on some stiff paper or on a background, perhaps cut from a magazine. Overlap the squares or glue them side by side.

◉ Exaggerate parts of the photo by using the same mini-image several times.

Indi, age 11

Morphing

If your school or family has a digital camera, experiment with photo-editing software to create **morphing** effects like these.

◉ Download some digital images onto your computer.

◉ Open an image with your photo-editing software.

◉ Click on the "effects" tab on the toolbar or see what choices drop down from the "edit" bar.

◉ Select and click on an effect. Your photograph will instantly transform itself!

Todd, age 8

original photo

oil painting

sketch

splash

melting

wrinkle

mosaic

emboss

fish eye

whirlpool

ribbon

spiral

ARTISTS AND ANSWERS

FAMILIES FOREVER (pages 4/5)

About WILLIAM HOGARTH

Hogarth (1697-1764) was an English artist who trained as an engraver. He then became a portrait painter but also painted comical pictures that told stories with a moral. He ran his own painting academy for 20 years and created the first permanent public gallery of English art. This was the main forerunner of London's famous Royal Academy.

About JACOB LAWRENCE

Lawrence (1917–2000) was an African-American artist, known for his pictures about the life and culture of black people in America. He painted portraits of black heroes and heroines, scenes of everyday life in the town of Harlem, and series of pictures showing both the achievements and the struggles of black people.

FAMILY FORTUNES (pages 6/7)

Answers for page 7

- The father indicates that his son will be his heir by pointing to him with his forefinger. The son also stands higher than his sisters and next to his father.
- The boy seems proud and haughty.
- The oldest daughter is the one next to the son. She has one foot on the platform and stands apart from the other two girls in a more active pose.

About ANTHONY VAN DYCK

Van Dyck (1599-1641) was born in Antwerp in Flanders (now Belgium). He trained as a painter from the age of 10. In his teens, he became an assistant to Rubens, the most famous Flemish artist of the time. His early pictures, of saints and Bible stories, were painted for churches. Later he traveled to England and Italy, where he worked on elegant, imposing portraits of kings, courtiers, and other important people. In London he became court painter to Charles I, who paid him a large salary and gave him a knighthood.

A FAMILY TREE (pages 10/11)

Answers for page 11

- Frida used a ribbon to link the family. Red suggests blood ties.
- Frida has added herself as a curled-up baby attached to her mother in the painting. In the photograph, Frida's father leans toward her mother.
- The strongest person is perhaps the father, who, together with Frida, is at the center of the picture and seems to shelter her. Frida cared deeply for her father.

About FRIDA KAHLO

Kahlo (1907-1954) was a Mexican artist. She started painting at the age of 19, encouraged by Diego Rivera, the famous Mexican mural painter, whom she married. Kahlo mainly painted people she knew, or self-portraits. In some self-portraits she wore bright Mexican clothes and included her favorite pet monkeys or birds. In others she showed images of her thoughts and feelings.

MODEL FAMILIES (pages 14/15)

Answers for pages 14 and 15

- Marisol's family is tense. None of the people touch one another and the father stands back. In Moore's family, the figures are close and intertwined.
- The upright stiffness and squareness of the figures makes them look serious and formal.
- The mother has a carved head, hands, and legs. The father's face and body are painted.
- The girl has three legs. The babies' feet are adult-sized.
- The buggy, the man's pant legs, and his shoes are ready-made. The head, hats, hands, and legs of the women and children are carved. The man's head and body and the woman's body are painted on wood.
- Moore was thrilled to be a father.
- Moore showed closeness by linking the parents' arms around their child.
- Moore's parents have small heads and almost no features. The curve of their backs is exaggerated, and their legs are very long. This creates a feeling of safety and protectiveness.

About MARISOL (ESCOBAR)

Marisol (b.1930) was born in Paris to Venezuelan parents. When she was 20, she moved to New York, where she still lives. Her sculptures are often inspired by photographs of ordinary people, especially families. These combine drawing and painting with carving and ready-made objects. She has also made casts of faces and limbs, arranged into artworks. Sometimes, she includes images of herself in her work.

About HENRY MOORE

Moore (1898-1976) was an English artist. He trained as a teacher before becoming a sculptor. The main themes in his work were reclining women and mother-and-child. Their shapes were often greatly simplified, sometimes with holes pierced through them. They were mostly carved in stone or wood. During World War II, Moore was a war artist and drew people in bomb shelters. As his fame and demand for his work grew, he started making large works for public places, which were usually cast in bronze.

FAMILY FEELINGS (pages 18/19)

Answers for page 19

- The furniture and carpet, fancy clock, decorated plates, gilt mirror, and gold candlesticks suggest wealth.
- Laure's pose is stiff and tense. Her expression is thoughtful and dreamy.
- No one in the picture looks at anyone else. This gives a feeling of tension and distance.
- Giulia's head turns toward her father and her body and foot are twisted toward her mother.

About EDGAR DEGAS

Degas (1834-1917) was a French painter who exhibited with the Impressionists – artists who were interested in painting scenes of modern life. Many Impressionists painted outdoors, trying to capture the effects of sunlight on a scene. Degas was more interested in movement and the effects of artificial lights at theaters and the circus. He captured dancers rehearsing as well as performing. He also painted scenes of horse races, women bathing, and portraits. In old age, when bad eyesight made drawing difficult, he modeled dancers and horses in clay or wax.

TWO OF A KIND (pages 22/23)
Answers for page 23

- The Cassatt picture shows a warm, close relationship between parent and child. The Raleigh portrait shows a stiff, more distant relationship.

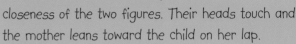

- Cassatt shows affection by the closeness of the two figures. Their heads touch and the mother leans toward the child on her lap.
- Raleigh wears a sword to show he is a soldier.
- Raleigh seems good-looking, dignified, and confident.
- Raleigh wanted his son to follow in his footsteps as an important soldier, so the son copies his pose.

About MARY CASSATT

Cassatt (1844-1926) was an American painter. She studied art in Pennsylvania and then in Paris, where she lived for the rest of her life. Her work was noticed by Edgar Degas, who invited her to exhibit with the Impressionists and later became a good friend. Cassatt mainly painted oil or pastel portraits of her family and friends, at home or at the theater.

THE FAMILY ALBUM (pages 26/27)
Answers for pages 26 and 27

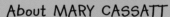

- Everyone is visible because they are at different heights – sitting or standing.
- The mother is the central figure in both cases.
- People are linked either with their arms or elbows.
- The oldest son and daughter stand nearest to the father; the mother is seated and positioned in the middle; they wear their best clothes.
- There are at least four pictures of each person's head.

- Hockney and the room are reflected in the mirror.
- The studio photos show still, solemn, and stiff families. Hockney's picture shows a more relaxed family in their own surroundings and gives a sense of action and lively conversation. It also includes pets.

About DAVID HOCKNEY

Hockney (b.1937) is an English artist who first became known as a painter. He is particularly famous for his portraits and interiors, which use strong, flat colors with a focus on light and reflections. He has also done stage designs for ballets and operas; made films; experimented with photomontages, fax art, and computer prints; and created many book illustrations.

GLOSSARY

coat of arms—a decorative emblem that is the symbol of a particular family

collage—a picture made by sticking bits of paper, fabric, or other objects onto a background.

family tree—a chart that shows how the generations of a family are related

generation—a family level; you are a generation below your parents, your children will be the next generation, and so on.

heir—the person who will take on, or inherit, the property of a dead person

morphing—to change an image, usually digitally

photomontage—a collage made up of photographs

portrait—an image of a particular person or group of people

pose—a physical position, or the action of getting into position (for example, posing for a portrait)

studio—an artist's or photographer's workplace

A First Look at Art

Places

Ruth Thomson

CHELSEA CLUBHOUSE
An Imprint of Chelsea House Publishers
A Haights Cross Communications Company
Philadelphia

This edition first published in 2004 in the United States of America by Chelsea Clubhouse, a division of Chelsea House Publishers and a subsidiary of Haights Cross Communications.

A Haights Cross Communications Company

Chelsea Clubhouse
1974 Sproul Road, Suite 400
Broomall, PA 19008-0914
www.chelseahouse.com

Library of Congress Cataloging-in-Publication Data applied for. ISBN 0-7910-7947-3

First published in the UK in 2003 by
Chrysalis Children's Books
The Chrysalis Building, Bramley Road,
London W10 6SP

Copyright © Chrysalis Children's Books, an imprint of Chrysalis Books Group, plc 2003
Text Copyright © Ruth Thomson 2003
Illustrator: Linda Francis
Photographer: Steve Shott
Consultant: Erika Langmuir, formerly head of education at the National Gallery, London

The author and publishers would like to thank the following people for their contributions to this book: Joanne Acty and children from Artworks; Jan Geddes, Richard Hutchinson, Michael Mitchell, Chris Miles and children from Laycock Primary School; Elizabeth Emerson.

Printed in China

Picture acknowledgements

Front cover: AKG London/© DACS 2003. 4: Bridgeman Art Library; 5: Bridgeman Art Library/©Estate of Stanley Spencer 2003. All Rights Reserved, DACS; 6/7: Bridgeman Art Library/©Estate of Grant Wood/VAGA, New York/DACS, London 2003; 10/11: Bridgeman Art Library/©ADAGP, Paris and DACS, London 2003; 14/15: National Gallery of Art, Washington, 1982.35.1/© ARS, NY and DACS, London 2003; 18: AKG London/©Estate of Stuart Davis/VAGA, New York/DACS, London 2003; 19: Alfred Stieglitz Collection, Fisk University Galleries/©ARS, NY and DACS, London 2003; 22: National Gallery of Art, Washington, 1970.17.45; 23: Bridgeman Art Library; 26/27: Bridgeman Art Library/© DACS 2003

10-05
23.00

Contents

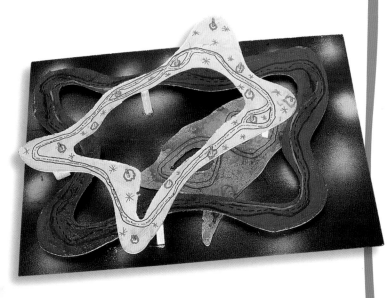

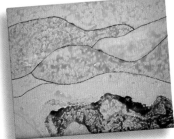

PICTURE A PLACE

Places have always inspired artists. Green countrysides, sunny coasts, and busy cities are just a few examples. In this book you'll see how some artists have portrayed real places, while others have worked from their imaginations. You'll find out what influenced the artists and learn about their techniques. We've included questions to help you look at the works of art in detail. There are also ideas for creating your own pictures and sculptures of both real and imaginary places.

◉ You'll find answers to the questions and information about the artists on pages 30 and 31.

Arty Tips

✰ Look for Arty Tips boxes that suggest handy techniques and materials to use in your own work.

Picture Hunt

✰ Picture Hunt boxes suggest other artists and artworks that you might like to find.

The Canal Bridge
L. S. Lowry
1949
(28 x 35.9 inches)

Cookham from Cookham Dean
Stanley Spencer
1938 (26 x 46.1 inches)

Choosing the view

When artists paint places, they make many choices that help them to create the right **atmosphere**. One thing they need to decide is a viewpoint. In the picture on the left, we look down a long city street. Lowry has painted it from high up – perhaps from the window of a building. Spencer's wide country valley, above, is viewed from a gentle, grassy slope.

Finding a focus

Artists also have to decide what details to include and emphasize in their scenes. Lowry's painting focuses on the road, with people trudging along it. Tall factory chimneys crowd the skyline and frame the picture on either side. Spencer's painting focuses on the open countryside. Lines of bushes and trees lead your eye in a zigzag to the faraway hills.

Color and mood

Artists can create certain moods by the way they use color. Grays and black darken Lowry's picture, suggesting a hard life in a smoky city. Calm greens and golds in Spencer's picture create a more peaceful atmosphere.

When you look at other pictures of places, think about the way that the artists felt about them. Would you feel the same?

5

A COUNTRY SCENE

Paintings of the open countryside are called **landscapes**. They are often shaped like this one, where the width of the **canvas** is greater than its height.

Open spaces

Artists can create landscapes that seem to stretch for miles. Follow the route of the horse and rider. See how the artist leads your eye along the winding road.

◉ What will the horse and rider pass on their countryside journey?

Into the distance

Notice how the road narrows in the distance. Eventually, it disappears at a point on the far **horizon** where the land meets the sky. This is known by artists as the **vanishing point**.

Stone City Grant Wood
1930 (30.3 x 40 inches)

An artist's tricks

The artist has used several other tricks to make things appear nearby or farther away.

See how objects that are bigger, bolder, and more detailed seem the closest to you. Things that are fainter, smaller, and higher up in the painting appear to be farther away.

Notice how things overlap. The line of dark trees on the left overlaps the hills. This makes the trees appear to be in front of the hills and therefore much closer.

⦿ Which windmill seems the farthest away?

⦿ Which building seems the nearest?

⦿ Which of the hills is most distant?

⦿ Which part of the painting seems closest to you?

LOOKING AT LANDSCAPES

From the hilltops

Stand on a hilltop with a wide open view and draw what you see.

◉ Concentrate on the outlines of buildings, trees, and shrubs that are both near and far away.

Molly, age 8

Kayla, age 8

Make a viewfinder

Artists often use a frame called a **viewfinder** to choose a good view. They hold it at arm's length and look through it to decide what to paint.

◉ Make a viewfinder of your own by cutting a rectangular frame from a piece of stiff paper.

Choose a view

◉ Use your viewfinder to select and draw a view. Add different **textures** for the ground, trees, and buildings.

Philly, age 7

Picture Hunt

✧ Compare works by some famous artists, such as John Constable, Claude Monet, Vincent Van Gogh, Paul Cézanne, and Camille Pissarro. Notice how they create a feeling of space, distance, and atmosphere in their landscape paintings.

A textured landscape

Make a **collage** picture of a real or imaginary landscape.

◉ Use materials that suit the place, such as real sand and shells for a beach; dried grass, flowers, or straw for fields; stones for a path or rocky shore; and twigs and leaves for trees.

Ned, age 7

Helen, age 9

◉ Or use scraps of fabric with different textures and patterns to represent hills, water, sky, and earth.

Model scenery

Create a 3-D model of a landscape.

◉ Use a piece of cardboard or stiff paper for the base, and paint it.

◉ Glue lumps of crumpled paper onto the base to make hills. Leave gaps between them for valleys.

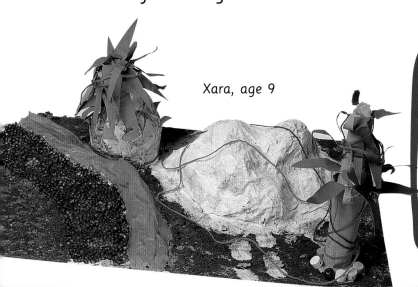

Xara, age 9

◉ Cover the surface with layers of papier mâché (see below) to create a smooth, rolling landscape.

◉ Use cardboard tubes for tree trunks and stick on leaves and flowers cut from colored paper or fabric.

Arty Tips

✫ Use craft glue for making collages.

✫ Mix craft glue with water to make papier mâché (use equal amounts of both). Dip torn paper strips into the runny glue and layer them at angles across one another for strength.

9

A PERSONAL PLACE

Sometimes artists are inspired by one particular place. Dufy, who painted this scene, was fascinated by the clear light and deep blue sea of Nice, on the south coast of France.

Admire the view

Here, Dufy invites us to come into his bright, sun-drenched room. Through the open windows we see a view of the sunny coastline that interested the artist so much.

◉ How does Dufy separate the room from the view beyond?

◉ What do you think the marks leading out from the right-hand window might show?

◉ How does Dufy show reflections and shadows?

Inside

The contrasting yellows and blues and the rich red carpet make Dufy's room glow with warmth. The white flowers bring a touch of the natural world indoors.

◉ How does Dufy show what is in the rest of the room, behind our viewpoint?

Outside

The lines of the French windows frame a fresh, airy view of the sea, sky, and town outside.

Notice how Dufy has painted things in the far distance very sketchily. The trees are black blobs, the bobbing boats are upturned V-shapes, and the buildings are just a series of lines and blocks of color.

Interior with Open Windows
Raoul Dufy
1928 (26 x 32.3 inches)

YOUR ROOM AND VIEW

Through the window

Draw or paint the view you can see from a window at home or at school.

◉ Cut a sheet of clear plastic wrap the same size as your picture. Lay it on top.

◉ Make a window frame to fit over the plastic wrap, using stiff paper or thin wooden strips. Glue the frame in place.

Samantha, age 11

Hermione, age 10

Shelley, age 11

Picture Hunt

✫ Compare Dufy's **Interior with Open Windows** with **Interior at Nice** and **Landscape Viewed from a Window** by Henri Matisse, or **The Breakfast Room** by Pierre Bonnard. Notice how they contrast the inside of a room with the scene outside.

◉ To suggest the room inside, stick the picture onto some wallpaper or onto a sheet of paper you have decorated.

Frame the view

Make a frame for one of your landscape pictures, so that you can hang it on a wall in your room.

◉ Lay your picture in the center of a sheet of stiff paper. Draw around the edges of your picture.

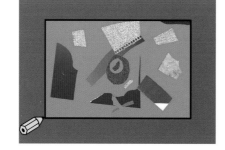

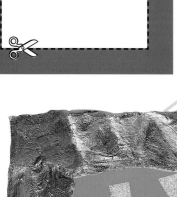

◉ Cut along the lines you have drawn.

◉ Paint and decorate your frame.

Khari, age 11

◉ Tape your picture to the back of the frame. Attach a piece of string so you can hang it up.

Arty Tip

✭ If you want to make a textured frame with raised patterns, glue some rolled or folded paper or some pasta, string, or shells onto the frame. Leave it to dry, then paint it or cover it with aluminum foil.

A shoebox room

Use a shoebox to create a room with a painted view or painted window.

◉ Cut one or more windows in the sides and/or base of the box.

◉ Paint the inside of the box to look like the walls, floor, and ceiling of a room.

Lucy, age 11

◉ Paint an outside view on a sheet of paper. Fit it across the window holes.

◉ Or paint a colorful pattern on some tracing paper, so it looks like stained glass.

◉ Tape the paper in place.

A PLACE OF EXCITEMENT

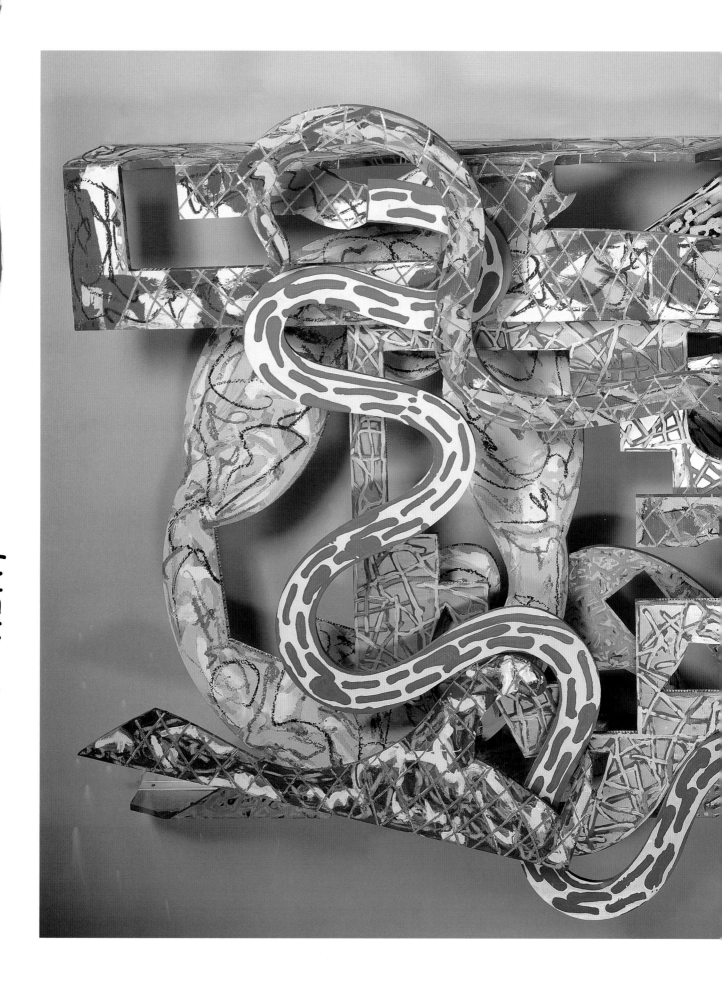

Jarama II
Frank
Stella
1982
(10.5 x
8.3 x
2.1 feet)

Artists don't always want to show what a place *looks* like. Sometimes they prefer to capture the *atmosphere* of a place, by suggesting what it feels or sounds like.

A roaring racetrack

In this work, Frank Stella shows the thrill he gets from watching roaring, zooming race cars speed around a track. The artwork, *Jarama II*, is named after a racetrack in Spain.

A tangle of metal

Separate, curving, painted metal tracks criss-cross one another here. They suggest the way race cars zig-zag back and forth when they overtake each other at top speed. The tangle of metal could also represent the dangers of car racing.

See how the pieces jut out from the wall at different levels? It's a cross between a painting and a sculpture. This kind of artwork is called a **relief**.

Imagine yourself at a racetrack while you look at this piece.

⊚ Follow the different colored tracks with your finger. How many tracks can you find?

⊚ Where do you think the race might begin or end?

⊚ Which marks resemble the smoke of car exhausts?

⊚ How does Stella represent the heat and noise of powerful car engines?

⊚ What do the dotted green lines remind you of?

CAPTURE THE FEELING

Zoom, zooooom!

Create your own roaring racetrack.

◉ Draw several racetrack ovals on stiff paper. Cut them out.

◉ Paint them with marks that suggest the speed and noise of racing cars.

◉ Paint a large sheet of cardboard or stiff paper for the background.

◉ Glue the racetracks onto the background at different levels. Use pieces of thick cardboard, foam, or dowels to separate the tracks.

Krystal, age 10

A thrilling ride

Make a collage of a spine-tingling ride, such as a Ferris wheel or a rollercoaster.

◉ Paint a sky on a piece of stiff paper.

◉ Use string, fabric scraps, and other materials to create your ride.

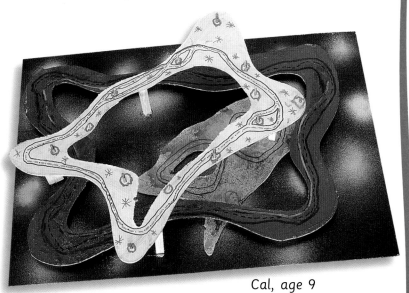

Cal, age 9

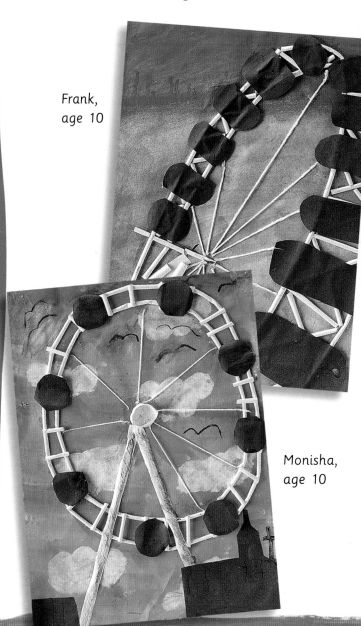

Frank, age 10

Monisha, age 10

Picture Hunt

✦ See how other artists have suggested the energy and excitement of a particular place or event, such as **Battle of the Lights, Coney Island** by Joseph Stella; **Eiffel Tower** by Robert Delauney; and **Montorgueil Street in Paris, Celebration of June 30, 1878** by Claude Monet.

Use all your senses

Think about what you see, hear, and feel in a favorite place. Imagine your home, a park, the sea, or an activity like a football game.

- Write down your sensations.
- Make a collage that expresses those sensations.

Home

Tomilayo and Zeynep

Enjoy the cozy atmosphere.
Feel the freedom.
Experience the fun.
Imagine the safety.
Feel the warmth.
Touch the comfort.

The concert

Musharrifaq, Abdul, and Chase

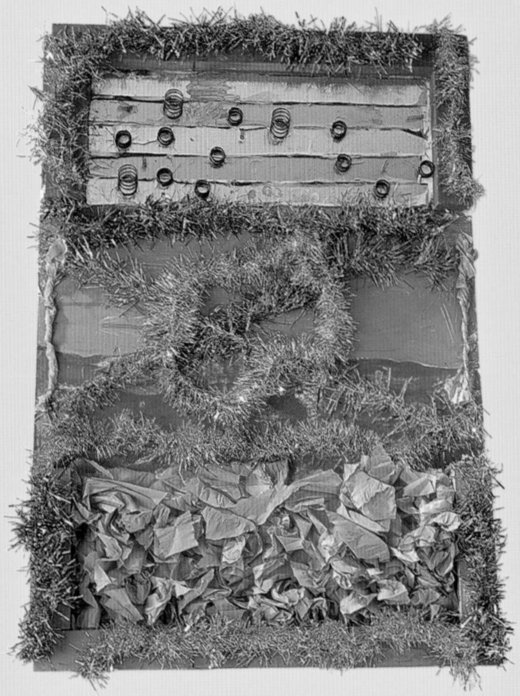

See the glittering lights shining in your eyes.
Feel the calmness building to excitement.
See the shadows of the singers
dancing on stage.
Feel the vibrations of the bass.
Hear the children screaming with excitement.
Feel your heart beating with happiness.
See the entrance door opening and closing.
See the people jumping up and down.
Feel the songs travel through your body.

Arty Tip

Use different materials to represent each feeling. In these two pictures the springs show excitement, the tinsel represents lights, the red fluffy material suggests warmth, and the curled paper expresses fun. What else could you use?

BRIGHT CITY LIGHTS

New York under Gaslight Stuart Davis 1941 (32 x 45 inches)

These two pictures show contrasting views of New York, a noisy, energetic city that is busy 24 hours a day.

Signs of life

For the painting above, Davis was inspired by the everyday sights he saw across the street from a shop. Notice the shop canopy stretching across the top of the scene with its handle hanging down.

Davis used a variety of shapes, patterns, and signs in clashing, sizzling colors to suggest the buzzing activity of city life.

◉ Is it day or night in Davis's picture? What two clues show you this?

◉ Can you find these shapes or patterns somewhere in the picture?

- zig-zags
- rectangles
- criss-cross grids
- stripes
- stars
- brick patterns

Radiator Building — Night, New York Georgia O'Keeffe
1927 (48 x 30 inches)

Twinkling tower

Here, O'Keeffe has focused on a single skyscraper. It had just been built when she painted it. The building towers above the rest of the city, with light from its top and windows gleaming brightly in the dark night sky.

O'Keeffe suggests busy city life by including beaming searchlights, rising smoke, and the glow of streetlights.

◉ How has O'Keeffe suggested the presence of lots of people in her painting?

◉ What colors has O'Keeffe used for the artificial city lights?

◉ How has O'Keeffe emphasized the great height of the skyscraper?

◉ Which of the two pictures do you think is better at capturing the feeling of a big city? Why?

NIGHT SIGHTS

The city skyline

⦿ Cut out shapes of skyscrapers and other buildings from black or gray paper.
⦿ Glue them onto a sheet of paper that you've painted dark blue.
⦿ Draw in lots of brightly lit windows using a soft white crayon.

Kerise, age 11

Khalida, age 11

Joel, age 8

Picture Hunt

✰ Look at these pictures by other artists who painted city scenes at night: **The Brooklyn Bridge** by Joseph Stella; **The Café Terrace at Arles at Night** by Vincent van Gogh; **The Boulevard Montmartre at Night** by Camille Pissarro; **Nighthawks** by Edward Hopper.

City silhouettes

⦿ Cut out some tall buildings from black paper. Cut holes for their windows.
⦿ Cut trees, people, and animals from black paper as well.
⦿ Arrange the pieces on a large sheet of tracing paper to create a busy city scene. Glue them in place.
⦿ Shine a light on the picture from behind, and admire the effect! A colored light bulb works well.

Shining lights

Use intense contrasts between light and dark to paint an exciting night scene that's glowing with bright electric lights.

- Paint the night sky either pitch black or very dark blue.
- Use strong, bright colors to make the buildings stand out.
- Use yellow or white paint for the beams or pinpricks of light.
- Outline any figures, or highlight parts of their faces in white.

Freya, age 11

Ella, age 11

Arty Tip

☆ Decide what direction the light is coming from in your scene. If it's from the left, highlight the left side of things, and so on.

SUNSHINE AND SNOW

The Artist's Garden at Vétheuil *Claude Monet*
1880 (59.6 x 47.6 inches)

Snow at Louveciennes
Alfred Sisley
1878 (24 x 19.9 inches)

Monet and Sisley were interested in the changing effects of natural light. They tried to capture on canvas an exact moment in time. They avoided using sharp outlines or precise details. Instead, they painted with dabs and dashes of color.

Heat and chill

In the painting on the left, Monet has created a sense of hazy heat. He used bright, contrasting colors that sizzle when placed side by side.

Sisley used a narrow range of drab colors to suggest the chilly feel of a gray winter's day.

◉ Which colors make one picture feel warm and the other feel cold?

◉ What time of day is it in Monet's garden? How can you tell?

◉ Why did the artists include people? Hide them with your finger. What difference does it make without them?

23

FEEL THE HEAT

Warm and cool colors

Red, orange, and yellow make us think of the sun, leaping flames, and glowing lights. These are known as warm colors. They can create feelings of energy and excitement in pictures.

Blue, green, and gray are known as cool colors because they remind us of ice, water, damp clouds, and chilly fog. Cool colors can create an atmosphere of calm, quiet, or gloom.

Picture Hunt

✫ Look at summery pictures of haystacks, harvests, and wheatfields by Vincent van Gogh. Notice the strong colors he uses.

✫ Look at other snowy scenes, such as **Hunters in the Snow** by Pieter Brueghel or **The Magpie** by Claude Monet, and wintery pictures by Hendrick Avercamp of people enjoying themselves on the ice.

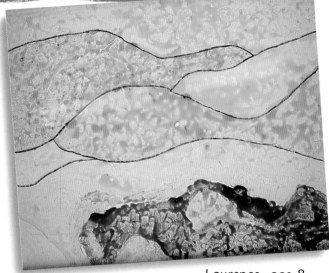

Laurence, age 8

Sun-drenched

◉ Draw a sunny landscape on clear plexiglass, using a permanent marker.
◉ Dab water-based glass paint on the plexiglass to create a textured surface.
◉ Put the picture in a place where light can shine through it and make it glow and shimmer.

Matthew, age 8

Ice-cold

◉ Use a variety of cool colors to paint a picture that will make people shiver when they look at it.

Seasonal collages

Make a collage that gives the feeling of a particular season.

◉ For the background, choose a color that is typical of the season you have chosen.

Spring

Kristina, age 8

Summer

Carolyn, age 12

◉ Cut out paper shapes that help show what the season is like. For example, long, spiky shapes might suggest winter icicles; petal shapes could suggest summer flowers.

Autumn

Camilla, age 12

Winter

Arty Tips

✩ Tear paper instead of cutting it, if you want a rough effect.

✩ Use shiny, patterned, and textured papers or fabrics, as well as plain colors.

✩ Put some of the shapes on top of one another to create layers.

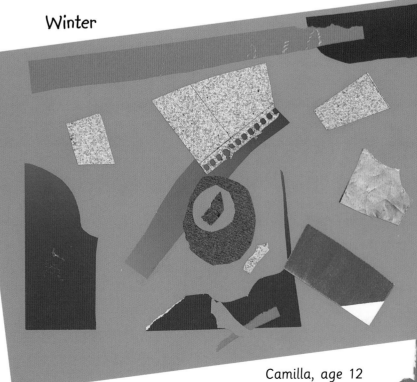

Camilla, age 12

AN IMAGINARY PLACE

Melancholy and Mystery of a Street
Giorgio de Chirico 1914 (34.6 x 28.3 inches)

Some artists paint the places of their daydreams. Giorgio de Chirico painted pictures of still, strange, silent cities. This one is full of puzzling features that invite us to ask questions. Who is the girl? Why is she in this place? Where is she going? Why is there an open train car here? Who is around the corner?

◉ Ask yourself questions and make up your own story about this picture.

A curious city

De Chirico included buildings from real places in his pictures – especially places in Italy where he lived. In the center of many Italian cities is an open square, often with the statue of a hero in it. Around the square are covered walkways called arcades, where people can stroll out of the sun.

Here, De Chirico hints at the view of a square, but he doesn't show it in a realistic way. The arcades and shadows are at odd angles, and we can see only the shadow of a heroic statue.

◉ What catches your eye first and draws you into the picture?

◉ Choose three words to describe the mood of the painting. How does it make you feel?

◉ What clue tells you that it must be a windy day?

◉ Where is the light coming from?

IN YOUR DREAMS

Strange roads

Create a strange, dreamy street
scene of your own.

Paris, age 11

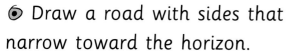

◉ Draw a road with sides that
narrow toward the horizon.
◉ Draw buildings on either side,
with walls that appear to become
smaller as they get farther away.
◉ Add some people and paint the
scene in dramatic, clashing colors.

Noah, age 11

Rio,
age 11

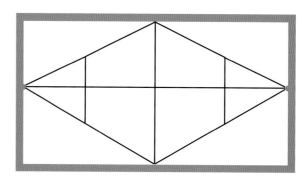

◉ Alternatively, draw two roads going
in different directions from the corner
where they meet.
◉ Draw a building on the corner, with
its two sides sloping toward the horizon.
◉ Paint something strange happening
on your weird and wonderful street.

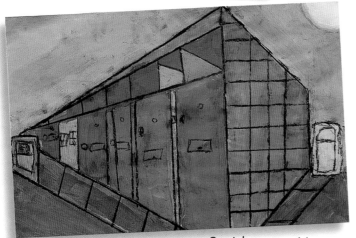

Conisha, age 11

Land of make believe

Paint a picture of an imaginary place. Think of answers to some of these questions before you start painting.

◉ What is the landscape like? Is it flat or hilly, grassy or rocky? Is it surrounded by sea? Are there waterfalls, volcanoes, craters, or canyons?

Meredith, age 8

◉ What grows in this place?
◉ What is the weather like?
◉ Who lives here? How did they get here? What do they look like? What do they live in? What is their lifestyle like?

◉ Think of a good name for your imaginary place. You could even create a map showing where the place is.

Arty Tip

✫ To make your pictures more dream-like, paint people and things in unexpected colors. Trees might have orange leaves, water might be pink, and people might have green hair or purple skin.

Freya, age 8

ARTISTS AND ANSWERS

PICTURE A PLACE (pages 4/5)

About L. S. LOWRY

Lowry (1887-1976) lived all his life near Manchester, a large industrial city in northern England. Many of his pictures are busy city scenes showing ordinary working people going about their everyday lives.

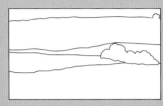

About STANLEY SPENCER

Spencer (1891-1959) was also an English artist. He is perhaps best-known for his imaginative pictures of Bible stories, set in the Thameside village of Cookham where he spent his childhood. He also painted many landscapes and portraits of himself and his family. During World War II, he was an official war artist.

A COUNTRY SCENE (pages 6/7)

Answers for pages 6 and 7

• The horse and rider will cross the bridge, passing a farm and windmill, then they'll go past a factory, a water tower, another farm, fields, and an orchard.
• The small windmill near the horizon seems the farthest.
• The red L-shaped barn seems the nearest building.
• The hill that is highest in the picture and nearest to the horizon line seems the most distant.
• The field at the bottom of the picture seems nearest.

About GRANT WOOD

Wood (1891-1942) grew up on a small farm in Iowa. His country childhood influenced a lot of his work, such as scenes of rolling farmland, views of village life, and humorous portraits of local people. Wood studied at art schools in America and traveled to Europe to visit galleries. His precise, crisp style was inspired by 15th century Flemish artists, who painted in a very clear and detailed way.

A PERSONAL PLACE (pages 10/11)

Answers for page 10

• Dufy separates the room from outside with the red carpet, the window frames, and balcony rails.
• The marks might indicate steps down to the beach.
• He shows reflections by adding dashes of white paint. He creates shadows using darker colors.
• The rest of the room is shown in the mirror.

About RAOUL DUFY

Dufy (1877-1953) grew up in the French port of Le Havre then moved to Paris. There, he was influenced by the paintings of Henri Matisse, who used unusually strong colors. Dufy developed his own style, using bright colors with sketchy outlines. He painted light-hearted, sunny scenes of the seaside town of Nice, as well as regattas (boat races) and horse races. He also illustrated books and designed fabrics and ceramics.

A PLACE OF EXCITEMENT (pages 14/15)

Answers for page 14

• There are nine different tracks.
• The race doesn't seem to have a definite start or finish.
• The white scribbly marks might suggest the smoke of car exhausts.
• 'Hot' colors (red, orange, and yellow) and jagged marks suggest the heat and noise of the cars.
• The green dotted lines could remind you of road markings, cars moving along the track, or speed marks.

About FRANK STELLA

Stella (b. 1936) is an American abstract painter. His early paintings were large canvases of black parallel lines with patterned bands of color. Later, he used shaped canvases, painted with colorful or metallic stripes that followed the shape of the canvases. He moved on to making painted, cut metal wall-objects (reliefs), and then to making huge cut-metal structures.

BRIGHT CITY LIGHTS (pages 18/19)
Answers for page 18

• The light in the shop and the moon in the sky show that it is night.
• There's a zig-zag spiral on the left; rectangles form signs, shop doors, bricks, windows, and skyscrapers; grids represent windows on skyscrapers, netting on the canopy, and the sides of a bridge; stripes are shown on signs, a flag, and a barber's pole; stars appear on the flag; brick patterns are on buildings and rubble.

About STUART DAVIS

Davis (1894-1964) was an American painter. His work was strongly influenced by modern city sights, particularly signs and advertisements. He was also inspired by jazz music. He used mainly strong colors and flat-looking shapes and often put words in his paintings.

Answers for page 19

• The lighted windows suggest the presence of lots of people.
• O'Keeffe has used white, yellow, orange, gray, and red for the artificial city lights.
• O'Keeffe has painted the skyscraper from below to emphasize its height.

About GEORGIA O'KEEFFE

O'Keeffe (1887-1986) was perhaps America's leading female painter. She was born on a farm in Wisconsin and decided early in life to become an artist. She painted American places, such as Lake George, New York, and New Mexico. She is also famous for her close-up paintings of flowers, bones, stones, and fruit.

SUNSHINE AND SNOW
(pages 22/23) Answers for page 23

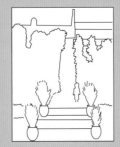

• Red, yellow, and orange make Monet's picture feel warm. Gray, blue, and white make Sisley's picture feel cold.
• It is probably late afternoon in Monet's garden, because you can see long shadows.

• The artists included people to lead your eye along the paths into their pictures and to give a sense of scale. Without the people, it would be difficult to tell how big or small the other objects in the pictures might be.

About CLAUDE MONET

Monet (1840-1926) grew up on the north coast of France. A local artist encouraged him to paint out in the open air, instead of indoors as most painters did. Monet then moved to Paris and befriended other artists, such as Alfred Sisley, Pierre Auguste Renoir, and Camille Pissarro. He persuaded them to paint outdoors as well. They developed a style known as **Impressionism**, named after one of Monet's paintings.

About ALFRED SISLEY

Sisley (1839-1890), a British artist, was born in Paris, France. He became friends with Monet and Renoir and painted with them in the countryside. He was among the group of artists that showed their work in the first Impressionist exhibition in 1874. Sisley spent his lifetime painting landscapes, gardens, and city scenes, but he had little success in selling his work.

AN IMAGINARY PLACE
(pages 26/27) Answers for page 27

• The girl, or perhaps the long white building, might have caught your eye first.
• You might choose the following words to describe the mood of de Chirico's picture: strange, mysterious, puzzling, unsettling, quiet, silent, spooky, chilly, scary, eerie, dangerous, alarming, odd, hushed. What other words did you think of?
• The flying flag shows that it must be a windy day.
• The light appears to come from both left and right.

About GIORGIO DE CHIRICO

De Chirico (1888-1978) was Italian, but he grew up partly in Greece. He trained as an engineer before becoming a painter. He is best known for his early paintings of mysterious dream-like cityscapes, drawn from real places. In his later life he worked in a more realistic style, painting mostly landscapes, Roman villas, and horses.

GLOSSARY

atmosphere—the feeling or mood of a place

canvas—a stiff cloth that artists use to paint on

collage—a picture made by sticking bits of paper, fabric, or other objects, onto a background

horizon—the line where the land meets the sky

Impressionism—an art movement in which artists painted out in the open air and focused on the effects of light

interior—an indoor scene

landscape—a countryside scene

relief—a raised artwork that is based on a flat surface; a cross between a painting and a sculpture

texture—how something feels to the touch, for example, rough or smooth

vanishing point—a point on the horizon where parallel lines (such as the sides of a road) meet

viewfinder—a frame used by an artist to pick a view

INDEX